Codes and Zones

Heather E. Schwartz

Consultant

Brian Allman
Principal
Upshur County Schools, West Virginia

Publishing Credits

Rachelle Cracchiolo, M.S.Ed., *Publisher*
Emily R. Smith, M.A.Ed., *SVP of Content Development*
Véronique Bos, *VP of Creative*
Dona Herweck Rice, *Senior Content Manager*
Dani Neiley, *Editor*
Fabiola Sepulveda, *Series Graphic Designer*

Image Credits: p6 Library of Congress [LC-DIG-stereo-1s05807]; p7 Library of Congress
[LC-DIG-stereo-1s11312]; pp8–9 Library of Congress [LC-DIG-hec-04117]; p10 Alamy/Naum
Chayer; p11 Alamy/Everett Collection Inc; p12 © Copyright The Carlisle Kid; p13 Library of
Congress [LC-DIG-ds-04874]; p16 Library of Congress [LC-DIG-matpc-03579]; p17 Library
of Congress [LC-DIG-ppmsca-56568]; p19 Library of Congress [LC-DIG-ppmsca-55692];
p20 (top) Library of Congress [LC-DIG-ppmsca-51737]; p20 (bottom) Library of Congress
[LC-DIG-hec-15268]; p23 (top) © British Postal Museum & Archive/© Royal Mail Group Ltd
2022 courtesy of The Postal Museum/Bridgeman Images; p23 (middle) Alamy/Jim West;
p25 (top) US Postal Service; p25, 29 US Postal Service; all other images from iStock and/or
Shutterstock

5482 Argosy Avenue
Huntington Beach, CA 92649
www.tcmpub.com

ISBN 978-1-0876-9111-4
© 2023 Teacher Created Materials, Inc.

Table of Contents

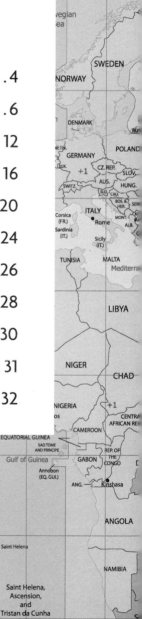

What Are All These Codes and Zones?

You have lived your whole life within the system of time **zones**. You probably dial area **codes** often. And you likely know what zip code you live in, too. But how much do you know about how these systems got started? Do you really understand how time zones, area codes, and zip codes work?

Most people may not know how they work, but they use the systems anyway without asking questions. They do not worry about why time zones set the time differently in other areas. They do not ask for reasons behind the numbers used for area codes. And they do not wonder why the post office needs people to use zip codes.

Maybe you did not have questions about time zones, area codes, and zip codes before, either. But now that we have brought up the subject, be honest. Aren't you a little curious to learn more? Dig into the history of these systems, discover how they work, and you will be an expert on topics few people know much about!

Code Confusion

Some people believe an area's zip code covers everything within the area. But that is not always true. A building that receives a lot of mail may have its own zip code separate from the area's zip code.

TIME ZONES*

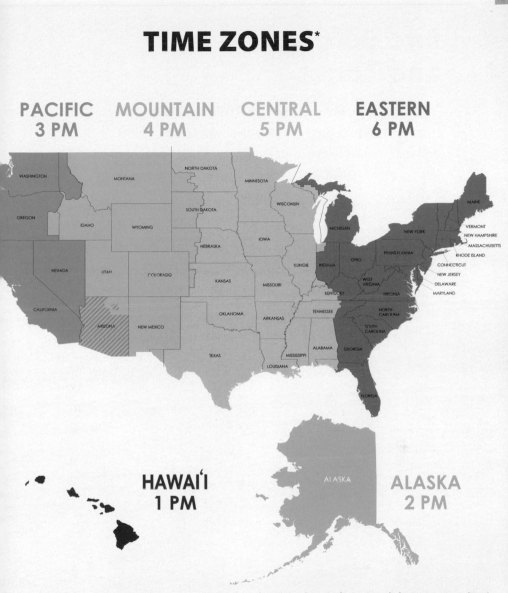

PACIFIC
3 PM

MOUNTAIN
4 PM

CENTRAL
5 PM

EASTERN
6 PM

HAWAI'I
1 PM

ALASKA
2 PM

Hawai'i and Arizona do not observe Daylight Saving Time (DST), which affects their time zones between March and November.

E64207468652060116F642069957A3
865206261736B65742E20486510D3
37265746C79207374616C6B735090
2206265686966E642074726565A32F
2757368657332C2073685275627145
16F642070061746368685132066F559

Life Before Codes and Zones

In the past, life was much different in the United States from how it is today. Before the late 1800s, for example, long-distance travel was not very common. It took several days to get to a new town or city on horseback or on foot.

Local time was different from town to town and city to city. In fact, there were more than 144 local times across North America. But it did not matter too much. People simply adjusted their watches and clocks when they arrived in a new place. It was an easy fix.

Washington, DC, 1899

travelers in Colorado, 1901

High Noon

Before time zones, local communities set their own time according to the sun. When it was at its highest point in the sky, that was noon. Each day, an official used the sun to set the time for the community.

Time differences became more difficult to manage as the railroad system developed. When people traveled by train, they got to faraway places much faster than in the past. They could still adjust their watches and clocks upon arrival. But sometimes, they got to a new town and realized the time was much earlier there than in the town they had left. This could make it seem like time was moving backward.

Time differences caused dangerous scheduling problems, too. Trains had to be scheduled to avoid crashes on the tracks. It was impossible to plan properly when each town and city kept its own time. Something had to change.

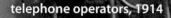
telephone operators, 1914

Phone Operators Place Calls

Communication was also much different in the United States in the past. The telephone was invented in 1876. Today, people use their phones all the time—and not just to make calls. Up until the late 1990s, however, phones could only be used to talk to other people.

In the early days of the telephone, placing a call took a few steps. You had to pick up the phone and talk to a **switchboard** operator on the other end of the **line**. You would tell the operator what number you wanted to call. They would make the connection for you.

In the early 1900s, phone numbers started with a word or letters to indicate the area. This was called the *exchange*. It was followed by four or five numbers to make each phone number unique.

Sometimes, things got confusing. Operators could not always understand what people were saying when they spoke. But they were more helpful than any **automated** system could be. Operators knew their community and the people in it. When calls went unanswered, they took messages. They even tried other numbers if they knew where someone might be.

But as more people started using phones more often, demand for operators grew. There were not enough of them to do the job. Something had to change.

Phones by the Numbers

In 1881, there were about 49,000 telephones in use in the United States. By 1948, there were 30 million phones. Today, there are about 455 million telephones being used across the country, including **landlines** and cell phones.

the first U.S. public post office, Philadelphia

Postal Service Grows

In America's earliest days, people stayed in touch by mail. They sent letters to faraway friends and family. But mail delivery was far from reliable. If someone wanted to send a letter, they had to ask sea captains and other travelers to carry their letters. They knew the letters might never arrive. Sometimes, they made several copies. They sent the same letter in different ways. It was the best chance they had to get a letter delivered.

Mail delivery started to get better in 1775. That year, the **colonies** established the U.S. Postal Service. In time, only postal workers handled mail. They sorted it depending on where it needed to go. They delivered it responsibly. By the 20th century, the system could handle more mail than ever before.

U.S. soldiers sort mail in France during World War II.

But then, World War II broke out. Many postal workers left their jobs to fight. Replacements took over. But there were not enough workers available to help. At the same time, people were sending more and more mail.

The system was overwhelmed. A new system was needed.

Mail Call

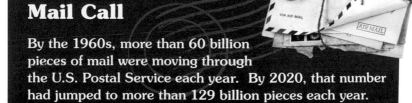

By the 1960s, more than 60 billion pieces of mail were moving through the U.S. Postal Service each year. By 2020, that number had jumped to more than 129 billion pieces each year.

Get in the Zone

One day in 1876, a man named Sir Sandford Fleming was traveling in Ireland and missed his train. The reason? The schedule had the departure time printed as p.m. instead of a.m. He spent what must have been an uncomfortable night at the station. Then, he decided to put an end to these kinds of mix-ups once and for all.

First, he started thinking up a system that would allow people to count the hours of the day in a different way. He thought it was confusing to count 12 hours in the morning and 12 hours in the afternoon. This gave him the idea to count time according to a 24-hour day.

Next, he took his idea a step further. He wanted to establish a **standard time**, which would be the same in entire countries and regions. Time would no longer change from town to town.

Train schedules played an important role in setting time zones.

London, late 1800s

Great Britain got on board with the idea in 1880. In the United States, Fleming's system had caught on at railroad stations by 1883. Standard time was not used throughout the country as law until 1918. Until then, some local areas kept their own time, even as the world changed around them.

Time for a Change

In 1900, Detroit still kept local time according to the sun. When the city council decided the city should switch to standard time, half the people there refused. The city did not make the switch until five years later. A sundial was used while the city tried to work out a switch to standard time.

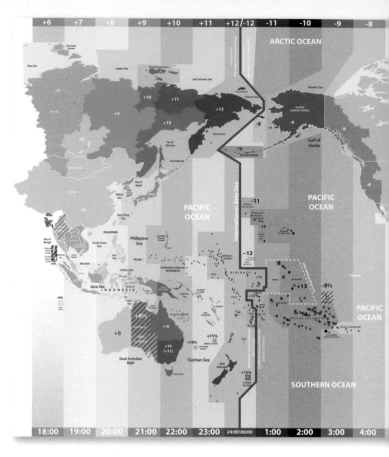

Time Zones in Action

Fleming's system made keeping track of time less confusing than it used to be. He created the 24 time zones that are used today.

It all began at the prime meridian. This is a **line of longitude** that divides maps and globes of Earth in half. Fleming set the starting point for standard time at the prime meridian. From there, he divided the world into 24 slices, using more longitude lines running from north to south. These slices held entire regions, countries, and states.

Each slice has its own time zone. The time is one hour different from one to the next. That means people around the world can recognize noon as the time when the sun is at its highest point in the sky. It also means the time remains the same in areas that are near to one another.

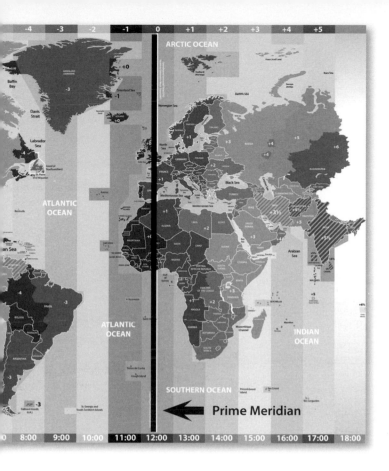

← Prime Meridian

8:00   9:00   10:00   11:00   12:00   13:00   14:00   15:00   16:00   17:00   18:00

In the **contiguous United States**, there are four time zones. From east to west, they are the Eastern, Central, Mountain, and Pacific time zones. U.S. time zones also include Alaskan, Atlantic, Hawai'i-Aleutian, Samoa, and Chamorro.

Daylight Saving Time

In most of the United States, the time changes periodically from standard time to daylight saving. Clocks are set ahead one hour in the spring to make the most of the daylight hours in the summer months. Then, in the fall, clocks are set back one hour again.

spring forward, fall back

Crack the Codes

Back in the 1940s, too many people were using telephones. There were not enough operators to place the calls. Robots were not an option. But automation was. If calls could be automated, the problem would be solved.

The Bell Telephone Company started working on a fix. The company created a system of codes. It was called the North American Numbering Plan. By 1947, North America was divided into 86 numbered areas. These were called *area codes*. At first, the caller told the operator the area code they wanted to call. Later, the caller could dial the number themself. They dialed the area code first. Then, they dialed the local phone number. They no longer needed operators. The calls went through automatically.

automatic telephone
exchange, late 1930s

Early Area Codes

The first area codes had three digits like they do today. But they always had a 1 or a 0 in the middle. That made it easy for early computers to tell the difference between area codes and local numbers.

telephone workers, 1979

In the early days, just one area code could cover an entire state. But today, there are many more phone numbers in use. Many people have landlines as well as cell phones. Tech devices, such as fax machines, watches, and tablets, might have their own phone numbers.

These days, there are more area codes than ever before covering smaller regions. The United States now has 335 area codes. More area codes help prevent duplicate phone numbers.

Computerized Calling

When automation started taking over, early phones had a **rotary** dial. It looked like a wheel with holes in it. Each hole showed a number. The caller turned the dial to input the correct phone number. If it was a long-distance call, an area code would be needed, too. The caller would hear distinctive clicks as the dial spun.

Today, most phones have a button dialing system. Both systems accomplish the same goal. They allow a caller to dial a number to make a call. Instead of reaching an operator, the caller reaches a computer. The computer reads the number to make the right connections. This helps the call go through.

When a caller dials an area code, that is a signal to the computer. The computer switches connections. It sends the call to another network covered by that particular area code.

These days, area codes are used for most calls, even those that are not long distance. If the area code is different from your own, you need to dial it. The phone number you are calling is in a separate network. The area code will tell the computer to make the switch.

rotary phone

poster supporting women telephone operators in the U.S. military, 1918

End of an Era

Some of the last telephone operators in the United States were still employed in their jobs until 2014. That year, technology finally took over, and AT&T eliminated its last operator jobs.

Zip into Zip Codes

The U.S. Postal Service faced a problem when workers went off to World War II. Replacements could not work as quickly to sort and deliver the mail. Plus, the volume of mail was increasing. There was more and more to be moved.

To keep up, the post office created a system that could help in large cities. It divided the cities into numbered zones. These one- or two-digit codes were placed between the city and state on pieces of mail. They made it easier for workers to sort the mail and send it where it needed to go.

postal carrier, 1957

a post office sorting room, early 1900s

This worked for a while. But over time, the post office was once again overwhelmed. Between the 1940s and the 1960s, the volume of mail doubled. Billions of pieces of mail were going through the post office each year. Zip codes worked in large cities, so the post office decided to expand the program.

In 1963, the Zone Improvement Plan (ZIP) divided the entire United States into numbered zones. Every address in the country got a five-digit zip code. Over time, using zip codes on mail became **mandatory**.

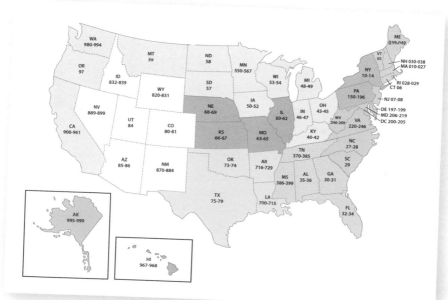

Inventor of the Zip Code

In 1944, Robert A. Moon was a postal worker with an idea. He thought the post office should use digits to code addresses. He is considered the inventor of the first three digits of the zip code.

Reading the Digits

Each number in a five-digit zip code has a purpose. It tells the post office where a piece of mail needs to go. The first digit indicates the region in the United States. The regions are numbered from east to west. For example, zip codes in Maine start with 0, while zip codes in California start with 9.

The next two digits send the mail to a central post office facility within the region. The last two digits tell which local post office should receive the mail. From there, it is delivered to the address.

Before zip codes, human workers had to sort all the mail coming through the post office. They had to decide where it should go next on the journey to its destination. Zip codes made automation possible. Instead of reading full addresses, workers could type zip codes into letter sorting machines. Today, machines can recognize the digits without any help. They use optical character recognition software.

3 2 4 0 2

ZIP CODE

clerks sort postal orders, 1934

postal workers at letter sorting machines, 1984

Zip Codes + 4

Mrs. Almita French
39 Berry Lane
Stanford, Ohio
35467-4567

In 1983, the U.S. Postal Service gave zip codes an additional four digits. These digits indicate an even more precise location where an address is located. But the system did not catch on, and they are still optional.

Convincing Customers

Time zones, area codes, and zip codes make life easier in many ways. But not everyone liked the new systems right away. When it came to time zones, for example, all U.S. states were in. Daylight saving time was met with resistance, however. Arizona opted out in 1967. Hawai'i quit in 1968. Both states had plenty of daylight year-round. People decided they did not need the hassle of changing their clocks twice a year. Some **U.S. territories** rejected daylight saving, too. These included Puerto Rico, the Northern Mariana Islands, the U.S. Virgin Islands, American Samoa, and Guam.

San Juan, Puerto Rico

Area codes caused an uproar for replacing place names with numbers. People felt they were cold and **impersonal**. Today, many people identify with the numbers that make up their area code. It stands for the place where they live.

Zip codes struck a lot of people as impersonal, too. The U.S. Postal Service had to create advertisements to convince people to use them. It took a while to work. But by 1969, they had made a difference. At least 83 percent of Americans were putting zip codes on their mail.

THE ZIP CODE DELIVERY NUMBER OF YOUR ADDRESS IS

10005

Include IT in Your Return Address AFTER the City & State

MR. ZIP

MAIL EARLY IN THE DAY!
YOUR POSTMASTER

The Ad Campaign

Some U.S. Postal Service ads in the 1960s featured Mr. Zip, a friendly cartoon mail carrier. Others included songs about zip codes and used snappy **slogans** such as "Put ZIP in your mail."

USE ZIP CODE THE LAST WORD IN MAIL ADDRESS

OUR ZIP CODE IS

Codes and Zones Work!

Time zones make travel easier and safer. Area codes allow there to be more phone numbers and let people make calls without an operator's help. Zip codes get mail moving faster to where it needs to go.

These codes and zones all do what they are supposed to do! Of course, it took time to get them right. They were developed and improved over the years. As things change, it makes sense to imagine that each system will eventually need upgrades. Otherwise, it will not be able to keep up with new technology and modern lifestyles.

Where will ideas for upgrades and improvements come from? From people like you! Now you know more about how time zones, area codes, and zip codes work. You will be ready to build on the past and dream up even better systems if they are needed in the future.

· New York ·

· London ·

· Frankfurt ·

·Hong Kong ·

· Tokyo ·

Always Improving

Are there too many time zones? Some scientists say yes.
They would like to set the time the same everywhere.
They think it would make things less confusing all around
the world, even though different times would involve
different sun positions depending on where you are.

Map It!

Zip codes help postal workers sort and deliver mail to specific areas. But they do not always have the same boundaries as the towns and cities they cover. Sometimes, landmarks within a town or a city have separate zip codes. Large cities may also have more than one zip code. Learn more about zip codes by creating a map of your area.

1. Create a map of the area where you live. Draw landmarks such as libraries, businesses, and schools. Include a few square miles (square kilometers) on your map.
2. Look up the address and zip code for each landmark. Write the zip codes next to the drawings on the map.
3. You may find that your area has only one zip code. Why do you think this is true? Think about the population and other reasons why there might be only one zip code.
4. You may find that the region you are covering uses several zip codes. If so, create a list of landmarks that fall in each zip code. Think about why the area is divided the way it is.

School

Church

Playground

Lighthouse
Museum

Glossary

automated—run by machines instead of having people do the work

codes—sets of letters, numbers, symbols, etc. that identify or give information about something or someone

colonies—areas that are controlled by or belong to a distant country

contiguous United States—the 48 adjoining states; also called the lower 48

impersonal—showing no interest in individual people, lacking emotional warmth

landlines—phones that are connected to the phone system by wires

line—a telephone connection

line of longitude—an imaginary line on maps and globes that goes from north to south

mandatory—required by law or rule

rotary—having a part that turns around a central point, like a wheel

slogans—words or phrases that are easy to remember and are used by a group or business to attract attention

standard time—the official time of a particular region or country

switchboard—a system used to connect telephone calls with many separate phone lines in a building

U.S. territories—areas of land under the authority of the United States but that are not states

zones—areas that are different from other areas in a particular way

Index

Learn More!

Sir Sandford Fleming was a creative problem solver. He may be best known for changing the way people think about time. But he also made changes to the railway system. He designed the first Canadian postage stamp. And he even invented an early in-line skate. Take time to learn about Sir Fleming. Then, follow these steps to celebrate his accomplishments:

- ✷ Research two to three of his inventions. Take notes describing what you find.

- ✷ Create a poster that includes information from your research. Include a picture of Sir Fleming on the poster.

- ✷ Draw more pictures and add captions to show his many achievements. Share your findings with your classmates.